WE CAN READ about NATURE!™
GOING PLACES

by CATHERINE NICHOLS

BENCHMARK BOOKS

MARSHALL CAVENDISH
NEW YORK

With thanks to
Susan Jefferson, first grade teacher at Miamitown
Elementary, Ohio, for sharing her innovative teaching
techniques in the Fun with Phonics section.

Benchmark Books
Marshall Cavendish Corporation
99 White Plains Road
Tarrytown, New York 10591
www:marshallcavendish.com

Photo Research by Candlepants, Inc.

Cover Photo: *Photo Researchers, Inc.*: Renee Lynn

The photographs in this book are used by permission and through the courtesy of:
Corbis: Royalty Free, 4; Laura Dwight, 5 (bottom). *Photo Researchers, Inc.*: Catherine
Ursillo, 5 (top); Art Wolfe, 7; George Holton, 10; Leornard Lee Rue, 13; Mark
Newmann, 19; Jerry L. Ferrara, 25; Stephen J. Krasemann, 27; Robert Maier, 28-29.
Animals Animals: Marcia Griffin, 8; Gerard Lacz, 9 (top & bottom), 16; Fritz Prenzel,
11(top); E.R. Degginger, 11 (bottom), Hans and Judy Best, 12; Paul Freed, 14; Michael
Fogden, 15, 18; Margot Conte, 17; D. Allan, OSF, 20, 21, 24; Anup Shah, 22; David
Barron,23; Leonard Lee Rue, 26.

Library of Congress Cataloging-in-Publication Data

Nichols, Catherine, date
Going places / by Catherine Nichols.
p. cm. — (We can read about nature!)
Includes index (p.32).
ISBN 0-7614-1252-2
1. Parental behavior in animals—Juvenile literature. 2. Animal locomotion—Juvenile
literature. [1. Parental behavior in animals. 2. Animals—Infancy. 3. Animal
locomotion.] I. Title. II. Series.

QL762.N53 2001   591.56'3—dc21   00-065122

Printed in Italy

1 3 5 6 4 2

Look for us inside this book.

baboon	cat
deer	frog
gibbon	gorilla
horse	kangaroo
koala	lion
opossum	orangutan
penguin	scorpion
sea otter	sloth
swan	tamarin
	tiger

When you were a baby,
how did you get around?
Were you pushed in a stroller?

Or held?

Or carried in a pack?

Animal babies need
to go places too.
Have you ever wondered
how they get around?

Emperor tamarin young with mother

When a mother cat needs to move her young, she picks it up by the scruff of its neck. This does not hurt the kitten.

Big cats carry their cubs this
way too.

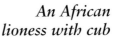

*An African
lioness with cub*

*A Bengal tigress
with cub*

Some animal young have their
own pouch.
They ride around inside.

A gray kangaroo with joey

Watch this joey climb in by itself!

This joey is grabbing a snack.

11

Some animal babies travel by piggyback.
This koala cub started out in a pouch.
Now it rides on its mother's back.

Wait for me!
An opossum baby scrambles
on board.

Baby scorpions are helpless
when they are first born.
Their mother carries them
on her back until they are ready
to go off on their own.

The tadpoles on this poison dart
frog's back cannot swim yet.
Their father will carry them like
this for a few weeks.
Then he will dive into water.
The tadpoles will swim away.

"Fall in line!" says the mother swan to her babies.

One cygnet is tired.
It hops a ride on its mother's back.

Sloths hang upside down in trees.
Their babies cling to them.

This mother sea otter floats
in the water.
Her baby rests on her chest.

Emperor penguins carry their chicks on their feet.

This penguin chick stays warm
under its father's thick skin.

Hold on tight!
That is what these babies do
when their parents swing from
tree to tree.

An orangutan and baby

A gibbon and baby

Some animal mothers cradle

A baboon holding baby

their babies in their arms.

A gorilla holding baby

Not every animal baby needs
to be carried.
This fawn is just a few minutes old.
Soon it will be able to stand and
follow its mother.

Sometimes it needs a push
to get going.

But with a little help, animal

babies are on their way!

fun with phonics

How do we become fluent readers? We interpret, or decode, the written word. Knowledge of phonics—the rules and patterns for pronouncing letters—is essential. When we come upon a word we cannot figure out by any other strategy, we need to sound out that word.

Here are some very effective tools to help early readers along their way. Use the "add-on" technique to sound out unknown words. Simply add one sound at a time, always pronouncing previous sounds. For instance, to sound out the word **cat**, first say **c**, then **c-a**, then **c-a-t**, and finally the entire word **cat**. Reading "chunks" of letters is another important skill. These are patterns of two or more letters that make one sound.

Words from this book appear below. The markings are clues to help children master phonics rules and patterns. All consonant sounds are circled. Single vowels are either long –, short ˘, or silent ⁄. Have fun with phonics, and a fluent reader will emerge.

When you come across a double consonant, make the consonant sound once.

s t r ō l l e r   s c r ŭ f f   k ĭ t t e n

g r ă b b i n g   w ĭ l l

The "ou" letter combination can make either of two sounds: the "ow" we say when we're hurt, as in ouch, or the "u" as in soup.

p o u c h   y o u   a r o u n d   o u t

30

A vowel at the beginning of a word can be either long or short.

ō̆ f f   ō p ŏ s s ŭ m   ē v e r_{rrr}

ā w ā y   ē m p e r o r_{rrr rrr}

The suffix –ed means that something already happened and sounds like either "d" or "t."

p ŭ s h ȩ d_t   c ā r r iē̆ȩ d_d   w ŏ n d e r_{rrr} ȩ d_d

t ī r ȩ d

- When a baby kangaroo is first born it is less than one inch long.
- When baby scorpions are first born they are wrapped in a sac. The mother scorpion rips the sac open with her tail, and the babies climb onto her back.
- After an emperor penguin lays an egg, the father takes over. He rolls the egg onto his feet and keeps it warm. For two months the father penguin watches over the egg. He doesn't eat until after the chick is born.
- Sloths live an upside-down life. They eat, sleep, and even give birth upside down.
- Sea otters do everything in the water. They even sleep there. So they won't drift too far, the mother sea otter wraps strands of seaweed around her and her pup.

glossary/index

chick	a young bird 20, 21
cradle	to hold in one's arms 24
cling	to hold on tight 18
cub	a young animal, such as a lion, tiger, or koala 9
cygnet	a baby swan 17
fawn	a baby deer 26
joey	a baby kangaroo 11
kitten	a baby cat 8
pouch	a pocket on the mother's body in which baby animals develop 10
scramble	to climb quickly 13
tadpole	a baby frog 15
travel	to go from place to place 12

about the author

Catherine Nichols has written nonfiction for young readers for fifteen years. She currently works as an editor for a small publishing company. She has also taught high-school English. Ms. Nichols lives in Jersey City, New Jersey, with her husband, daughter, and their pet Moonlight, a white cat with a long black tail.